OIL RIG ROUGHNECK

By Geoffrey M. Horn

Reading Consultant: Susan Nations, M.Ed.,
author/literacy coach/consultant in literacy development

Gareth Stevens
Publishing

Please visit our web site at **www.garethstevens.com**.
For a free catalog describing Gareth Stevens Publishing's list of high-quality books, call 1-800-542-2595 (USA) or 1-800-387-3178 (Canada).
Gareth Stevens Publishing's fax: 1-877-542-2596

Library of Congress Cataloging-in-Publication Data

Horn, Geoffrey M.
   Oil rig roughneck / Geoffrey M. Horn.
      p. cm.—(Cool careers—adventure careers)
   Includes bibliographical references and index.
   ISBN-10: 0-8368-8883-9   ISBN-13: 978-0-8368-8883-6 (lib. bdg.)
   ISBN-10: 0-8368-8890-1   ISBN-13: 978-0-8368-8890-4 (softcover)
   1. Offshore oil industry—Employees—Juvenile literature. 2. Offshore oil industry—Vocational guidance—Juvenile literature. I. Title.
   HD8039.O34H67   2008
   622'.338023—dc22   2007027665

This edition first published in 2008 by
Gareth Stevens Publishing
A Weekly Reader® Company
1 Reader's Digest Road
Pleasantville, NY 10570-7000 USA

Senior Managing Editor: Lisa M. Guidone
Managing Editor: Valerie J. Weber
Creative Director: Lisa Donovan
Designer: Paula Jo Smith
Cover Photo Researcher: Kimberly Babbitt
Interior Photo Researcher: Susan Anderson

Picture credits: Cover, title page © Reza/Getty Images; p. 4 Reinaldo D'Santiago/AP; p. 5 Donna McWilliam/AP; p. 7 © Steve Starr/Corbis; p. 8 Map Resources; p. 9 Chitose Suzuki/AP; p. 10 Map Resources; p. 11 Oleg Nikishin/Getty Images; p. 13 Jim Sanchez/AP; p. 14 Map Resources, © George Steinmetz/Corbis; p. 15 Rob Stapleton/AP; pp. 16–17 Ira Block/National Geographic/Getty Images; pp. 18–19 Al Grillo/AP; p. 21 Map Resources, Manoocher Deghati/AFP/Getty Images; p. 22 Map Resources, AFP/Getty Images; p. 24 Dave Cauklin/AP; p. 25 David McNew/Getty Images (top), Paul Sancya/AP (bottom); p. 26 © George Steinmetz/Corbis; p. 27 Map Resources; p. 29 Paul Sakuma/AP

Printed in the United States of America

1 2 3 4 5 6 7 8 9 10 09 08 07

CONTENTS

Words in the glossary appear in **bold** type the first time they are used in the text.

CHAPTER 1

HUNTING FOR OIL

The biggest treasure hunt in the history of the world is happening right now. This treasure doesn't gleam like gold. It doesn't shine like diamonds. It's sticky, greasy, and smelly — but it's worth trillions of dollars. This treasure is called crude oil.

Gasoline comes from crude oil. So does jet fuel. Without crude oil, airplanes couldn't fly, and army

Crude oil is pumped from Lake Maracaibo in Venezuela, the top oil-producing country in South America.

Without jet fuel from crude oil, this aircraft could never leave the ground.

tanks would come to a dead stop. Crude oil is also the source of thousands of other products. Bubble gum, deodorant, credit cards, crayons — they all come from crude oil.

Oil rig workers pump crude oil around the clock. People rely on the oil industry to produce as much oil as the world needs. This isn't easy. The world's thirst for oil increases every day.

A Growing Thirst

During the early 1970s, the world used about 50 million **barrels** of oil each day. Today, the daily total is about 85 million barrels. The United States uses more oil than any other country. Each day, Americans use almost one-fourth of the world's output of oil. China and Russia also use large amounts of oil. So do Germany and Japan. These two nations buy almost all their oil from other countries.

Some of the oil used in the United States is found close to home. States like Texas and Alaska are big oil producers. So is the Gulf of Mexico. Large amounts of oil are found in the "tar sands" of Alberta, Canada. In these tar sands, the oil is mixed with sand, clay, and water.

The United States, Canada, and Mexico hold about 16 percent of all the world's oil. The rest is found in more distant places. Many of these areas are difficult and dangerous. Some of the world's oil comes from war zones — for example, Iraq. Oil is also taken from the deserts of Central Asia and the icy waters of the North Sea. Wherever oil is found, oil rig workers will pump it.

Danger in the Delta

Each day, the United States imports about a million barrels of oil from Nigeria, a country in Africa. Most

Rigs and Roughnecks

An oil rig pumps oil out of the ground or **seabed.**
At the heart of the rig is the drill. The drill cuts
through rock to reach the oil. A **derrick** supports the
drill. It looks like a metal tower, narrow at the top and
wide at the bottom.

The word *roughneck* has been used since the
1830s. When it first appeared, it meant "thug" or
"bully." The word took on a new meaning in the early
1900s as the oil industry grew. Oil rig workers were
called roughnecks because they had to be strong.
The work they did was dirty and hard.

Today, *roughneck* usually means a member of the
drilling crew. It can also apply to any oil rig worker.
A few roughnecks are women, but most are men.

Three roughnecks work the
drill on a Lake Maracaibo
rig in Venezuela.

of Nigeria's oil is found in the Niger Delta. Unfortunately, the Niger Delta has become a very dangerous place for oil workers.

Oil has made a few Nigerians very wealthy. But most of the people are very poor. They blame the government for not making their lives better. They accuse the oil companies of paying big **bribes** to government officials. They also blame the companies for hiring foreign workers instead of Nigerians. Drilling in the delta has polluted the region's air, water, and soil.

In recent years, some Nigerians in the delta have formed armed gangs. These gangs target foreign oil workers. In February 2007, gunmen shot and killed an oil worker from Lebanon. Many other foreign workers have been kidnapped. The oil companies have paid large **ransoms** to set them free.

The oil firms say that they have helped people in the Delta by building roads, schools, and hospitals. But the armed gangs may force the companies to pull out. The violence has hurt the country's oil industry. It has made life harder for the oil workers — and for the people of Nigeria.

Over a Barrel

The most common way to measure crude oil is by the barrel. A standard barrel of oil holds 42 gallons (159 liters). Back in 1970, oil cost less than two dollars a barrel. Today, a barrel of oil may cost up to eighty dollars or more.

After crude oil is taken out of the ground, it is shipped to a **refinery.** A refinery is a special kind of factory. The refinery turns crude oil into gasoline, jet fuel, heating oil for homes and businesses, and other products. In 1970, a gallon of gas cost about thirty-five cents. Today, the price is more than two dollars a gallon. That's more than a whole barrel of crude oil cost in 1970!

CHAPTER 2

DRILLS, THRILLS, CHILLS, AND SPILLS

People have been using crude oil for thousands of years. The first oil wells were dug in China more than sixteen hundred years ago. But the great worldwide hunt for oil did not begin until much later. The first modern oil well was dug at Azerbaijan, near Iran, in 1848. Eleven years later, a successful well in Pennsylvania launched the U.S. oil industry.

Gusher!

The oil boom reached all the way to southeast Texas on January 10, 1901. Two drillers, Al and Curt Hamill, were working on a well at Spindletop Hill. They had been drilling there for weeks but had found nothing.

Suddenly, mud began bubbling up from the well. Then, tons of drill pipe exploded out of the hole! The workers ran for their lives. A few minutes later, a giant jet of oil began shooting out of the ground.

Spindletop gushed oil for nine whole days. Finally, workers capped the well and got the oil flow under control. Soon, the well was producing 100,000 barrels of oil a day.

Spindletop was the biggest **gusher** that the world had ever seen. News of the thrilling discovery spread far and wide. People flocked to Texas to try to strike it rich. These oil seekers were called **wildcatters.** It might take a lot of equipment — and funds — to drill a well. If they struck oil, they could earn a lot of money. If they hit a dry hole, they could lose everything they owned.

Oil rigs and a TV tower mark the skyline near Baku, the capital of Azerbaijan. The country is located north of Iran.

Big Oil

Sometimes, wildcatters knew what they were doing. More often, they based their drilling on guesswork. They failed much more often than they succeeded.

Today's oil drillers are different. They base their decisions on science. They carefully study the kinds of rocks that are likely to hold oil. They make detailed maps of the layers of rocks on land and beneath the sea. They use advanced drilling methods. Often these oil drillers work for big companies. These big oil firms can afford to send drill crews anywhere in the world.

The Thunder Horse oil rig in the Gulf of Mexico is the world's largest floating oil platform.

Oil firms like Exxon Mobil, BP, and Royal Dutch/Shell rank among the biggest companies in the world. Exxon Mobil took in more than $370 billion in 2006. The company made a profit of almost $40 billion — a new record for any U.S. company.

"Rock Oil"

Crude oil is often called **petroleum.** This term combines two old Latin words, *petra* and *oleum.* *Petra* means "rock," and *oleum* means "oil." Petroleum is oil that is found in or below rocks or soil.

Fossil Fuels

Crude oil is a **fossil fuel.** *Fossil* comes from the Latin word *fossilis*, which means "dug up." Fossil fuels like oil and coal are very old. The oil and coal we use today took millions of years to make.

Fossil fuels began as plants and animals that lived in the ocean. When they died, they fell to the bottom of the sea and were covered in mud. The thick, heavy mud pressed down hard on the decaying matter. As the pressure increased, heat built up. The heat and pressure changed the dead plants and animals into the sticky stuff we call crude oil. Coal formed in a similar way.

Harsh Conditions

Big oil companies operate oil rigs in some of the world's hottest places — and some of the coldest. One of the richest oil regions in the United States is also one of the coldest. This area is Prudhoe Bay on Alaska's North Slope. The North Slope is near the Arctic Ocean.

The Alaska pipeline took two years and $18 billion to build. It was completed in 1977.

Crews worked hard to clean up after the 1989 Exxon tanker oil spill, but parts of Alaska's coastline are still polluted.

Winters are harsh. For two months, the sun never rises. Temperatures drop as low as –60° Fahrenheit (–51° Celsius). When the wind blows, it feels much colder.

A huge oil field was discovered at Prudhoe Bay in the late 1960s. Several big companies got together to build a pipeline to carry the oil. The pipeline runs 799 miles (1,286 kilometers) from Prudhoe Bay to the port of Valdez. From Valdez, the oil is shipped to other U.S. ports by huge ships called **supertankers.**

Oil is very important to Alaska's economy. But it also poses a threat to the state's environment. In 1989, an Exxon tanker spilled more than 250,000 barrels of oil. The oil polluted Alaska's coastline. The disaster killed many birds, fish, and sea otters. Damage from the oil spill can still be seen today.

CHAPTER 3

WORKING ON A RIG

At least five thousand companies in the world drill for oil and natural gas. In the United States, more than 300,000 people work in the oil- and gas-drilling industry. Many thousands of others work on pipelines and in refineries.

Workers on a drill crew must be in good physical shape. They work long hours in all kinds of weather. The equipment they use gets greasy and dirty. Often, they must spend weeks at an oil field far from home.

Roustabouts and Roughnecks

On an oil rig, the lowest-paid workers are the **roustabouts.** They do much of the dirty work. They move and paint equipment. They load and unload supplies. They help keep the rig clean and safe.

Many kinds of oil workers are called "roughnecks." But on an actual work crew, roughnecks usually handle the drilling equipment. The drill may need to grind through hundreds of feet of rock to reach the oil below.

Three roustabouts do much of the heavy lifting on this oil rig in the Gulf of Mexico.

Each drill starts with a hollow steel pipe. At one end, the pipe is connected to a motor. This motor turns the pipe around and around. At the other end, the pipe is connected to a drill bit. The metal in the bit is very hard. The bit grinds through the rock.

Looking for weak spots, crews use special equipment to check oil transit lines near Prudhoe Bay, Alaska.

As the drill pushes deeper and deeper into the ground, more pipes need to be added. The roughnecks connect new pipes to the drill. Over time, the drill bit wears out. When that happens, roughnecks pull out the pipes and attach a new bit. Roughnecks earn more than roustabouts because they have more skills.

The Higher-Ups

Other workers on an oil rig have special skills and earn much more money. For example, motorhands can earn more than twenty dollars an hour. Motorhands are in charge of the motors used on the rig. One motor turns the drill pipe. Another motor may raise and lower it.

The person who manages the whole rig is called the toolpusher. The toolpusher gives orders to another skilled worker — the driller. The driller manages the drill crew.

A Few Words About Gas

The word *gas* has many different meanings. It can be short for *gasoline*. This is the fuel you put in the gas tank of a car. A refinery turns crude oil into gasoline and other products.

The word *gas* may also mean "natural gas." Natural gas is a fossil fuel. It is often found when people drill for crude oil. The United States has a large supply of natural gas. Many Americans use it for cooking and for heating their homes.

The derrickhand helps the driller and watches over the derrick and the drill. Derrickhands have one of the more dangerous jobs on a rig. They spend much of the time near the top of the rig — on the monkey board. This narrow platform is attached to the derrick. It's 90 feet (27 meters) or more above the drill floor. Derrickhands can't be afraid of heights. They may need to wear a safety harness. If they fall, the harness will stop them from hitting the ground.

Wild Wells

Work on an oil rig can be dirty and dangerous. It's even more dangerous when a well goes wild.

Some wild wells are **blowouts.** A blowout occurs when oil or gas blasts out of a well. (This is what happened at Spindletop in 1901.) A huge blowout can hurt or kill the workers on a rig. It can also damage equipment. When a blowout takes place beneath the sea, oil pollutes the ocean and nearby shore.

A fire on an oil rig can be very dangerous — but only if it gets out of control. Often, oil workers will start a controlled fire to burn off unwanted gas that is found along with the oil. This kind of controlled fire is usually very safe. But a fire that starts from a sudden spark may put the oil workers in grave danger. They may die from an explosion, extreme heat, flames, and fumes.

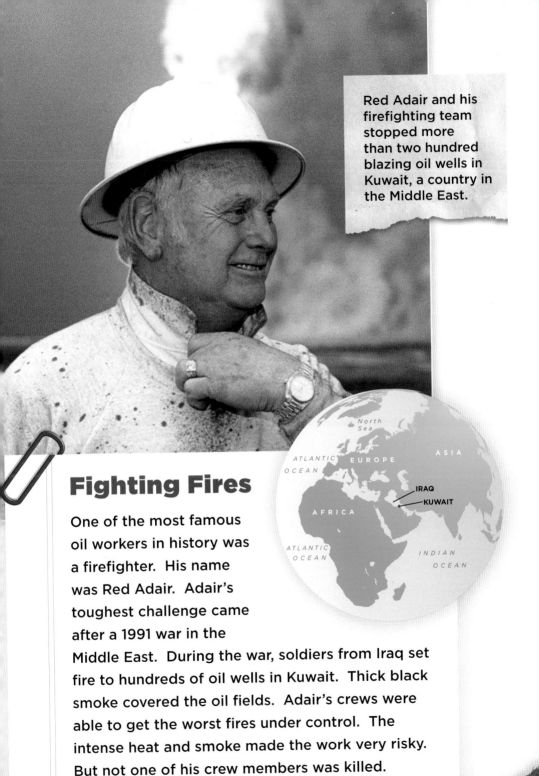

Red Adair and his firefighting team stopped more than two hundred blazing oil wells in Kuwait, a country in the Middle East.

North Sea

ATLANTIC OCEAN

EUROPE

ASIA

AFRICA

IRAQ

KUWAIT

ATLANTIC OCEAN

INDIAN OCEAN

Fighting Fires

One of the most famous oil workers in history was a firefighter. His name was Red Adair. Adair's toughest challenge came after a 1991 war in the Middle East. During the war, soldiers from Iraq set fire to hundreds of oil wells in Kuwait. Thick black smoke covered the oil fields. Adair's crews were able to get the worst fires under control. The intense heat and smoke made the work very risky. But not one of his crew members was killed.

CHAPTER 4

THE CRUEL SEA

Much of the world's oil is found **offshore.** A major source of U.S. oil is the Gulf of Mexico. Great Britain gets much of its oil from the North Sea. Many North Sea oil rigs are a long way from land.

To find oil at sea, rigs based on large platforms drill deep into the seabed. Near each rig is another platform, where oil workers eat, rest, and shower. This platform serves as a floating hotel — a "**floatel,**" some people call it.

Daily Life on an Oil Platform

Life is not easy for North Sea oil workers. In 2005, a worker named Andrew Johnson talked with a reporter about his job. His usual workday was twelve hours long, he said. Most often, he spent two weeks at the drill site, then two weeks on land. Johnson's work involved climbing high on the rig. His job was to check for weaknesses in the steel structure. He spent much of the day in a safety harness. He knew the work was dangerous. But he said the job had an "excellent safety record."

What did the oil crew do to relax? They could watch DVDs, work out in a gym, or play table games and bingo. Tobacco was allowed in indoor smoking areas — never outdoors, because of the danger of fire. Alcohol and drugs were strictly banned. If you were in a fight, you could lose your job.

A helicopter ferried workers back and forth between Scotland and the North Sea oil field. What was the best part of Johnson's job? "The helicopter ride home," he joked.

An oil company in Norway built this large North Sea rig.

When Disaster Strikes

The North Sea can be a cruel place to work. In March 1980, strong winds sent waves crashing into a platform east of Dundee, Scotland. Many workers were watching a movie when the floatel collapsed. In all, 123 people lost their lives. Later, investigators found a disturbing fact. One of the platform's metal legs had a crack. The crack made the leg break when the waves hit.

The worst offshore oil disaster in history took place in July 1988. It happened on another North Sea platform — the Piper Alpha. This oil rig was poorly maintained. It had a gas leak, which caused a terrible fire. A total of 167 workers were killed. Some died in the blaze. Others died when they tried to escape the fire by jumping into the sea.

Smoke pours from the remains of the Piper Alpha oil platform in the North Sea off the coast of Scotland, where 167 workers lost their lives.

From Oil Rig to Gas Pump

About two-thirds of the crude oil used in the United States comes from other countries. Some of it is brought in from Canada and Mexico. But much of it comes from faraway lands.

Let's follow a barrel of North Sea oil. How might it move from an offshore rig to a gas pump in the United States?

1 On a North Sea rig, workers pump the oil from beneath the sea.

2 The oil enters a long pipeline that links the rig with a terminal on land.

3 At the terminal, the oil is pumped onto supertankers.

4 A supertanker carries the oil across the Atlantic Ocean. It may take two weeks to reach the United States.

5 The supertanker docks at a special oil port. There, the oil is pumped into another pipeline.

6 The pipeline carries the oil to a refinery. At the refinery, the oil is made into gasoline and other products.

7 Tanker trucks haul the fuel to the gas station. There, the fuel is held in underground storage tanks.

8 The fuel is pumped into the gas tank of your car!

CHAPTER 5

IN THE HOT ZONE

Hot? You don't know what hot is until you come to Abqaiq, Saudi Arabia. Here in the Middle East, desert heat is a fact of life. In summer, the daytime temperature can hit 140°F (60°C). Rainfall is rare — only a few inches each year.

And why would you want to come here? The answer is simple. Saudi Arabia sits on top of about 20 percent of the world's oil. Much of that oil passes through Abqaiq.

Abqaiq is a hot target for **terrorists.** They don't like the Saudi government. They think the Saudi royal family ruling the country is **corrupt.** They also believe Western countries and oil companies have too much influence on the government and its policies. Terrorists tried to blow up the Abqaiq oil plant in February 2006. Experts think they may try again.

A controlled fire burns excess gas at an oil field in Saudi Arabia.

Oil and Global Warming

All fossil fuels contain carbon. When they burn, some of the carbon joins with the oxygen in the air. That forms a gas called **carbon dioxide.**

Trees and other green plants take in carbon dioxide and produce oxygen. People and animals breathe in oxygen and breathe out carbon dioxide. All of this is a normal part of nature. But too much carbon dioxide can lead to big problems. Carbon dioxide and some other gases cause changes in Earth's climate. These gases are making our world warmer.

When we burn more and more oil and coal, we add to global warming. Global warming will make the oceans rise. This may cause floods and other disasters. Scientists think we can reduce global warming by cutting our use of fossil fuels.

Trouble in the Desert

Security is serious business in Saudi Arabia. Three electric fences surround the Abqaiq plant. Thousands of armed guards stand ready to defend it at all times. Helicopters and F-15 warplanes patrol the area twenty-four hours a day.

The Saudi government also keeps a careful watch on Ras Tanura. This city is the home of the largest **oil terminal** in the world. Each day, it stores or ships up to 50 million barrels of crude oil.

Other Saudi cities are not as well guarded. On May 1, 2004, terrorists struck the oil city of Yanbu. They shot and killed five foreign oil workers. A worse attack took place in Khobar later that month. The terrorists hit an area where many foreign oil workers live. The gunmen killed twenty-two people.

War in Iraq

Oil workers face even greater danger in another Middle East country — Iraq. For decades, Iraq was one of the world's top oil producers. A brutal dictator named Saddam Hussein ran the country. The United States led an invasion of Iraq in March 2003. Within a month, troops had forced Saddam to flee.

The war damaged Iraq's oil industry. Some people thought the oil industry might recover quickly. It didn't. Instead, different groups of Iraqis began fighting over who would control the nation's oil. Hundreds of attacks have been carried out. Many pipelines in Iraq have been blown up. On March 30, 2006, masked gunmen attacked a bus carrying oil workers. Eight of the workers were killed.

In Iraq, as elsewhere, oil workers understand the dangers they face. They work long hours under difficult conditions. They know their job — to find and pump the oil we need. Our job is to use it wisely.

If all these vehicles used less fuel, the world's oil supply might last longer.

Running Out of Oil

Crude oil takes millions of years to form. But we are using it up at a rapid rate. Everyone knows the world's oil supply can't last forever. In fact, some experts think the world will start running out of oil in the next ten or twenty years.

Oil workers are doing their best to keep the oil flowing. What can the rest of us do to conserve it?

- Drive cars that use less gas.
- Don't waste electricity. Turn off lights when we're not using them. Buy new kinds of lightbulbs that consume less power.
- Support the use of energy sources that won't run out. These include power from wind and sunlight.

GLOSSARY

barrel — in the oil industry, a measure equal to 42 gallons (159 liters)

blowouts — powerful blasts of oil or gas from wells

bribes — payments made to persuade others to take improper or illegal action

carbon dioxide — a gas produced when fossil fuels burn

corrupt — dishonest and not to be trusted

derrick — on an oil rig, the metal tower that supports the drill

floatel — short for a floating hotel

fossil fuel — a fuel, such as crude oil or coal, produced over millions of years from the remains of dead plants and animals

gusher — a well that produces huge amounts of crude oil

offshore — at a distance from a country's coast

oil terminal — a place where oil is shipped and stored

petroleum — another name for crude oil

ransoms — money paid or demanded in exchange for the freedom of a person who has been captured

refinery — a factory where crude oil is turned into gasoline, jet fuel, and other products

roughneck — in general, a worker on an oil rig; more specifically, a member of the crew that handles the drill pipes

roustabouts — the lowest paid and least skilled workers on an oil rig

seabed — the ocean floor

supertankers — huge ships designed to carry crude oil

terrorists — people who use threats and violence to force others to meet their demands

wildcatters — people who search for oil on their own, usually in untested areas

TO FIND OUT MORE

Books

Career Ideas for Kids Who Like Adventure. Career Ideas for Kids (series). Diane Lindsey Reeves and Nancy Heubeck (Facts on File)

Fossil Fuels: A Resource Our World Depends On. Managing Our Resources (series). Ian Graham (Heinemann Library)

Oils and the Environment. Resources (series). Ian Mercer (Stargazer Books)

What If We Run Out of Fossil Fuels? High Interest Books (series). Kimberly M. Miller (Children's Press)

Web Sites

American Petroleum Institute
www.api.org/story
Click on the links for videos explaining how oil is found, produced, transported, and refined.

Captain Platform Virtual Visit
resources.schoolscience.co.uk/SPE/index.html
Tour a North Sea oil rig.

EIA Energy Kid's Page: Energy Facts, Fun, Games, and Activities
www.eia.doe.gov/kids
Learn more about how oil was formed and where it is found.

Howstuffworks "How Oil Drilling Works"
science.howstuffworks.com/oil-drilling.htm
Find out more about the science behind exploring and drilling for oil.

INDEX

About the Author

Geoffrey M. Horn has written more than three dozen books for young people and adults, along with hundreds of articles for encyclopedias and other works. He lives in southwestern Virginia, in the foothills of the Blue Ridge Mountains, with his wife, their collie, and six cats. He dedicates this book to all scientists, public officials, and private citizens working to reduce the world's dependence on fossil fuels.